WHEEL SPIN

E K Macdonald

abuddhapress@yahoo.com

ISBN: 9798862472400

For A.G, P.H, W.H.C, S.A, L.H and C.D.H who all loved a road trip but reached their destination too early. RIP.

Table of Contents

*Denotes previously published stories (see end for details)

HANGAR STRAIGHT
(2012 Ferrari F430 Coupe)

The instructor inspires me with confidence. The way he handles his helmet and slides into the seat. He looks through his mirror glasses like he's seen hundreds of me reflected hundreds of times before.

I grin at him because I want him to like me. I want to be cool but I'm clumsy getting into the car. I fumble with the harness and muddle the straps.

He unravels me. I wince at my girlish giggle, but he ignores me and plugs my clip points secure. My hands tremble on the wheel, and I say 'oh' and 'fuck' when I realise, I need to grapple with paddle-change gears. I paw on the pedals and listen, awed by the engine's throbbing bass beat.

"Don't worry about what's behind you," he says, seeing me glance in the mirrors like I'm driving in town. "Concentrate on your racing line. Just do what I say."

I listen to his instruction. I want to impress. I follow his 'keep left' and 'now right hand down' and 'find your apex point' and 'change up, change down, accelerate, balance the car, steer through the blind brow, a highly technical section,' and 'here's a tight right hander, slow for this ninety-degree turn. Hangar Straight now, the fastest part of the course. Like that? Stowe Corner—be patient with the power, it's longer than you think,' and as we speed past the start line again, 'faster' he says, 'you know the track now. Take it faster this time.'

And I start to relax. My confidence grows and I frown and concentrate on holding my line. I concentrate on driving like I'm told.

He tells me to pull into the pits so he can go through it again. He says, imagine the track, picture its bends and chicanes, its straight lines, and corners.

"Remember," he says, "spot your apex points." He flicks his hand forward. "When you go through the Loop before Hangar Straight, the adverse camber means you have to balance the car." His hand is held out flat and he tilts it from side to side like a French man saying, *comme ci, comme ça.*

"Align your wheels before you accelerate. Otherwise, you'll spin out of control." I follow his finger, pointing upwards and spiralling fast with his hand.

"Now," he says, "you're racing this time."

I try to dismiss the thoughts of crashing or skidding or spinning or flipping. I drive onto the track, scowling in concentration.

I spot and watch and let the revs roar back at me, thunderous and growling complaint and I'm driving hard and fast and corners rear and slither like snakes, and I wrestle for control, flick my fingers through gear changes, brake and accelerate and he's shouting at me to wait, wait! as I drive out of the loop, and straighten the car onto Hangar and then he's shouting,

NOW! NOW!

FOOT DOWN, ALL THE WAY!

GO!

GO! GO! GO!

And I'm stepping down hard and I sense the needle winding the dial as the straight disappears, under the burning wheels and I'm driving so fast, so damn fast and I'm wanting to brake and wanting to brake and he's saying not yet, not yet, hold it, wait, wait, and the engine is roaring and the corner is rearing, racing towards me and I want to trust him though I tussle with excitement and extreme exhilaration and power and fucking flying freedom and furious fast fear so, so blissful and my children's faces and my wanting to live...

WAIT!

But I brake. And I know I disappoint him for losing my nerve. For puncturing my own bravado—bottling it—and choosing safety first. And I feel deflated as I sense his interest in me wane.

He removes his helmet and takes off his gloves to shake my limp hand. He compliments my driving, like he's instructed to do. I see myself mirrored in his glasses, in all my red-faced sweating shame. I see a reflection of who I really am.

KISSING IN A BOTTLE GREEN JAG
(1974 JAGUAR XJ6)

Father said he didn't care when he saw Mother kissing. Didn't
care then—didn't care anymore—when he saw her illuminated,
kissing her bearded lover in the bottle green Jag.

Mother didn't know—or did she? —he'd be walking the dog.
Alone on the dusky lane except for the faithful companion.

Perhaps the car was seductive when they leaned back to
drive, admiring their reflections in polished walnut, and
shining vanity mirrors. When they reclined in soft, yielding, kid
leather seats.

I guess we children were tucked up in bed, sleeping in the
dark, quiet house. We must have been left quite alone.

PARK OUT IN ANDALUCÍA
(1985 BMW318i)

She drives them out, speeding on the Marchena road. Carmona, the sentinel town is fortressed high behind them, the closer slopes an infantry of olive trees. She feels the eyes of the town watching them, senses eyes everywhere in their eagerness not to be seen.

She races the car over the plain. Sun-tanned wheat puckers with shadows from rare clouds, like slow bruises on tender skin.

Ángel doesn't own a car, doesn't drive, but he shows her where to go. The plains, so flat from above, have hollows, shallow gullies, baked banks of crumbling clay.

She pulls in where he indicates with his lit cigarette. She realises—he's been here before. They park-up behind a stand of gnarled and knotted trees. The sandy siding sparkles with tossed beer-can rings, cheap gems of smashed glass, cigarette butts and flimsy cellophane.

They leave the car doors open, both front and back. Hot breaths of wind lift her skirt, redden her face. The leather sticks to the backs of her bare legs.

Afterwards, Ángel lights up. She watches through narrowed eyes, now despising his fast-flicking hands, his quick, and his lazy actions.

He shakes out the ashtray, tips butts onto Carmona's midden. Five thousand years of waste flung over walls, tossed to lie layered beneath five-fingered sticky figs or pinioned under barricades of prickly pears, baring their pimpled, swollen pink fruits.

Ángel slams his door.

"Vamos!" he says. He points to the road, looking straight ahead.

She drives, slower this time, testing him and showing him patience.

They enter Carmona via the Cordoba gate. She senses being watched again, though she no longer cares.

She pauses to let Ángel out of the car, lets him use the eyes of the town as an excuse not to kiss her. She hears his casual farewell, three hand slaps on the car roof. She watches him stride away with his rolling hip walk then slip faster, towards the narrow street corner and sees, he's trying hard not to run.

OVERSEAS EXPERIENCE
(1983 Nissan Sunny)

They watch the strangers pick over, weigh, value, and price their belongings. Jon counts the few precious bucks they've earned from their saleable stuff.

Kelly gives away clothes, a few dog-eared books. She packs tea-chests to store under Jon's parent's house, over on the North Shore.

Jon sells his Spider surfboard. He doesn't want to, but they need the cash. They sell the Valiant too, though keep the roof racks, and Jon's Mum lends them her Nissan to get about.

Back south in Onehunga, they hold their leaving party in the now empty house. The stripped, echoing rooms give plenty of space to darken and dance in. They drive to get there over the spanning bridge, arching high above the water. White hulled yachts confetti the dark sea and ferries sidle across the harbour. The two frigates moored at Devonport look like toys, taken from a battleship game.

There's graffiti on the underside of their motorway exit. It always makes them laugh. 'Land rights for Gay Whales.' It appeared around the same time as 'Don't drink and drive home. Smoke dope and fly home.' They're not big smokers—can't afford much—but once grew a bit of their own. The bushy plant was nicked just as it was swelling fat, sticky with resiny buds, taken over the back fence—a beer crate ladder left behind like an insolent calling card.

The darkened rooms soon jam with sweaty, mostly familiar faces, illuminated in glimpses by light bubbles climbing the walls and onto the ceiling. The music is fast and loud. Smoke hazes above tossing heads, beers bob in buckets of melting ice. The heavy guys hang on the back porch, sucking on a bong, hassling each other. Jon is with them.

Kelly dances, arms over her head. She takes deep swigs from offered bottles, thinking she's quenching her thirst. She hugs friends who shout over the music, like they mean it, "We're going to miss you!"

"I'll miss you too," Kelly shouts but she doesn't mean it either. Jon says two years, but Kelly thinks she might be leaving for good. Might become one of those people who only returns for temporary visits, weddings maybe or to see the old folks for Christmas.

When the party dwindles, some leave in shared taxis, some walk, most people drive though they shouldn't. Jon and Kelly move with exaggerated care. They pile the stereo and speakers, an unsteady jumble, in the back of the car.

Jon says he's so stoned he's flying, so Kelly takes the seat at the wheel. She drives hugging the kerb, crawling along until joining the motorway. Jon hangs out of the window and sings with his eyes closed, his voice croaking from too many smokes.

The signs on the harbour bridge can confuse Kelly even in daylight. Red crosses marking closed lanes, green ticks for open, managing traffic flow. Lanes like liquorice laces, tied and tangled, and coloured neon signs, dazzling if looked at long enough.

Kelly panics. The red crosses and green ticks, the black lanes shuffle, and twist. She swerves between lanes, fighting to maintain control in the unfamiliar car. She stretches her eyes open, looks but doesn't see, and drives onwards, climbing with the rearing, buckling, steel-straddling bridge. High, flying, overseas. Gone and away, leaving for good.

PLUCKY BACKPACKERS IN THE LYNMOUTH FLOOD
(1947 Austin A40)

If you read the report from 1952, they call us 'plucky'. It's a word the English use to describe Australians. Something to do with pioneering grit. The way we face obstacles square in the face, stare them down like a cow cocky seeing off a tricky-minded steer. The way we face 'harsh' and the creatures who might kill us if the dry don't get to us first.

Pluck wasn't enough. If you read on, you'll see it says, 'both sucked into oblivion.' Sounds to me like pioneering of a different kind. Like heading for outer space. I can say fair and square, it's not the adventure Gwenda and I had in mind.

We plucky girls wanted to see the old country. Our mothers, they wanted us to learn some grace and manners from home.

"Polish off the hard edges," my Ma said.

"A diamond is still a diamond in the rough" my Da might have said but he never said much at all. 'Na' or 'Yip' is about all you could expect, but he'd narrow his eyes when Ma talked about England as home.

On the voyage over we had nothing to fear except the boredom and the seasick. Surrounded by water for weeks we became used to the moods of the sea. Colours changing from steel grey to green, to oily flattened glass and white-tipped blue. The swell and sink of the waves, shuddering humps then sulking gullies. It seems a joke now, my guts heave-ho in the ocean, waiting for the rest of me to come. Benign seas, stretching thousands of miles when a few twisting river streams became the striking snakes with forks in their tongues.

Gwenda and I had the travel bug. We wanted to see for ourselves the green and pleasant land. The emeralds and limes. The fresh watery hope of it, so quaint and easy after cracked earth and brittle-blue mountains and silver-kindling brown gums.

We liked an oak standing in milk-rich pasture. Barrels of beeches, brambles in hedgerows and hand-built stone walls. We liked yew trees in churchyards where the gravestones of Jones's and Smiths leant into the grass. We liked villages with wells and thatched cottages, topiary chickens and chess pieces and close mown cricket pitches and lawns.

We were plucky when we stuck out our thumbs. We liked the way drivers stepped on their brakes and swerved as they turned to look at us. We jiggled on hard suspension in backfiring lorries, sat on the fenders of a tractor towing a trailer of pigs. We took rides in cars slipping their gears and once shared a seat—Gwenda perched on my knee—in an open-top racer driven at scream-out-loud speed.

Gwenda and I were thick, though like petty thieves we scrapped over small things which don't matter. Gwenda had an eye; she liked a tickle and tease. She said I could be hostile, off-putting with men.

"Just enjoy yourself," she'd say. Well, she was right. If we knew what was coming, we'd all live a whole lot more. Sometimes I think I'd have done more, sooner, and faster. Sometimes I think I'd have slowed right down.

He was called Tony, the young man who gave us the last lift. Gwenda stuck out her hand, thumb pointing up and curling back like a hook. Tony was a good-looking fella. Thick black hair and straight brown eyes. I sat in the back like usual and Gwenda sat up front, side-on to him as she chatted. I kept my eyes on the road—Tony, getting distracted, needed the help.

We were glad of the lift. The weather had turned, and the wind couldn't make up its mind. Coming from this way and that like bluebottles flying in for a feed. The sky was darkening, purple bruised, and I could see it was going to rain yet again. Not the usual English dribble-and-mist but real rain. The kind that falls like a bucket tipped over your head.

Tony said it wasn't too far to drive us there though I could see he wished it was. He knew the guest house above a river in a place called West Lyn Valley. The hills rising to the moor rolled black with the sky and the rain started to fall when we ran inside. Gwenda was laughing when she waved goodbye. Rain always made her happy. She said she liked the wet of it and she stretched her arms to the sky.

The rain—it kept coming. More than a bucket over our heads. More like a dam bursting, spilling, and slicing in sheets. The trees jawed and cracked when we peered out of the windows, but we couldn't see much. We helped to roll flour sacks at doors to keep out the water and it's true, we plucky girls felt scared when we turned in for bed. We'd seen heavy rain before but not like this for so long. It was the sound that went with it. Like an animal's roar. Like the roar of an animal breaking free from a trap. Or going in for the kill.

We were taken in our beds. Pencil narrow cots with pricking pillows and mean blankets. We clung to them like rafts in the crashing collapse and slide and grind and tear of tree roots and iron and bricks and glass and dark and spark of fused car lights, chair sticks and ticking and doors torn from hinges and tiles shorn in the spit and sludge and sink and slurry. And we went with it, thrown out like dirty from the floor-washing bucket to gape and bulge like bugs in the mud, bloated and floating face down out at sea.

We plucky girls were plucked from the water. Too late to bring back from the brink. And the oblivion they talked of? I'll tell you it has a silence of its own. As quiet as my scattered ashes in the sun-baked yellow back home.

AIRCOOLED VW BAJA
(VW Baja Beach Buggy)

Step 1: Raise the beetle and remove the wheels.

For a modest man, you like a car to attract attention. Oily blackness lies under your nails, dots, and spots your face, inking your skin. You show me your manual.

Ten easy steps, "Sweet as".

      You flick your fingers then slide, skating away on your trolley so only your lower legs protrude from under the car.

Step 2: Remove the engine cover and the rear bumper.

A car that says surfer, off-roader, mechanic, Mad Max.

Step 3: Take off the running boards and the rear fenders.

That says dunes and Sex Wax, sand tracks through marram grass.

Step 4: Undo the throttle cable and remove wires.

Riptides and swell, the resin of pine trees from Muriwai
Woodhill spit-sticking on the off-shore wind.

Step 5: Cut off the rear apron.

Escape the apron strings, you say as if that's supposed to be
funny. Exposed and essential. Emissions as raw as roll bars.
Essential roll bars — so it turns out.

Step 6: Take out the engine from the engine bay.

Remove everything surplus, take out the back seat and floor
mats. Remove the muffler.

Make some noise. Listen to the engine reverberate. Practice
brace and acceleration in an empty downtown car park, just to
hear that sound. Ricocheting off concrete, echoing deep into
underground recesses.

Should practice brace more than acceleration.

Step 7: Mark out and cut the fenders to shape.

Flared for fats. Clearance to slide on tight corners. You're in a
tight corner boyfriend, ten easy steps—I repeat back what you
said.

Step 8: Remove the welds.

Customised for driving from Kawhia to Raglan, airborne over hot black iron sands.

Step 9: Reinstall and reconnect the Baja Bug engine.

Air cool. Cool as wrap 'round, black shades, you dude. Air cool the inside out hot engine.

Step 10: Put the fat wheels back on the Bug.

Blonde. Suspension of summer, with a slab of cold beer.

Suspended upside down on slip-sliding sand. Wind switches

and surf booms and thunders. Exhausted hot pipes burn me,

searing a deep-reminding scar.

IN THE CANNON OF BEECH TREES

(1970 Morris Minor Traveller)

They stop often. Stops for the whining dog. Stops for Daddy to climb a fence to 'see a man about a dog,' stops because one of the girls feels sick. For picnics by a beauty spot or in a summery field. Sour milk and tea from a leaking thermos. Warm sandwiches, slipping apart, cheese skidding on cucumber.

Daddy snoozes, his hat covers his face. Milly makes daisy chains then fidgets, mithering him, tickling with blades of grass.

There are stops for antique shops, for Tintern Abbey or Chepstow. For petrol or beans on toast at Knife-Fork and Spoon motorway breaks. Sometimes the girls bed down in nylon sleeping bags, rolling side by side under blinking lights.

They play eye spy and count crunched-over bikers— their jackets puffed up with air like Michelin men. The girls call them baddies when they roar past the car and feel the thrill of being afraid.

Milly likes to sing. 'She'll be Coming Round the Mountain', 'Morning has Broken', 'What Shall We Do with the Drunken Sailor'. Daddy joins in, but tires before Milly. She sings into the wind, her fine hair tickling her face, streaming tears.

Clare draws or writes secrets in her diary. Milly tries to peek, but Clare snaps her diary shut and holds it tight to her chest.

Sometimes Clare imagines having a scythe extended from her window, slicing everything level in its path. Hedgerows and road signs, trees, and telegraph poles, all tidy and neat.

At some point, Mummy and Daddy argue, a small annoyance that grows sore. Daddy drives on grimly, reaching behind to pat the girl's legs. Mummy ugly crying for miles. Her face blotchy, eyes pink under swollen lids.

"Let me out! Go on without me!" She threatens to open her car door.

They're canyoning through a tunnel of green beech trees when she does—she opens her door. There's a tussle and shouting, the car swerves. The girls wide-eyed, begging for Mummy to stop. With sudden braking, the car skids to a halt and Clare's pencils and secret diary fall into the footwell. Her white socks drop to her ankles when she stamps with angry feet.

DEAD CENTRE
(1992 Hallbilt MFG Tri Axle Log Trailer)

The day is perfect for what we have in mind. Whiteout, frozen, dry cold like ice and rye.

I argue with Hank though I know he won't listen. We agreed to have the bike pedal to sit smack in the centre. Right on the road's median line.

"Jesse, not everythin' in life is symmetrical. It's more disruptive if it's not dead centre."

Hank has the camera. He holds it one handed, like he's some pro. I place the bike, so it lies fallen on its side, black frame, and black wheels over the salted black road's white line. Like abandoned.

"More," says Hank. "It's cool to be off kilter." Hank always wants more.

The hoar frost trees bend towards the tarmac but can't reach—frozen before full extension. The air is thick and white, and our breath, it clouds our faces and fogs up the view finder.

Hank steps back from the bike and takes his shots. He steps to one side of the road, then the other, then stands, just off centre as if the circlet shape in the distance, made by the tunnelling bent trees, is his focus.

I stamp my feet to keep warm, clapping my gloves. I keep look out. Scanning for car lights, the blaze of double-trailer trucks coming out from Franklin Lake Mill, but I know we'll hear before we see them, grinding through the gears. The snow dampened damn quiet makes every sound louder.

The camera shutter clicks. Hank straightens up. "Here, hold the camera."

He picks up the bike, wheels it to the side of the road and pushes it, to skate through the ice fringed dogwood, so it's hidden from view. I'm not sure what he's doing but I have a sick feeling I'm not going to like it.

Hank returns to the road and lies down on the salted grit. I'm still checking for cars and trucks knowing something will come along soon.

Hank has always liked an edge. He likes going too fast and getting too high. He's the one to walk furthest out on the lake, closest to the water hole on the thinnest ice. Hank always says that risk—gettin' real close to the edge— makes him feel most alive.

He lies there, not dead centre, but like near to it, on the right-hand side of the midline. On his back, head pointing towards the white light circle in the far distance, arms pinned tight by his side, streamlined, like he's planning to fly.

"Shoot," he calls to me. "Get all angles, front on and by the side."

I'm not liking this much. Him lying there, not flying but looking like he's some kind of roadkill. It don't sit easy with me. Still, I shoot. Front on, side on, all angles.

When I hear the truck, I'm saying, "Time to move Hank. Get your arse off the ground!" Then I'm shoutin' and hollerin'.

"Hank move your arse. Stop fuckin' with me!" And all he's saying is keep shootin' the pictures.

He lies there, even when we have visual. We don't just hear it and feel it, but see it too, and Hank he won't budge, just still as ever and shoutin,' "Keep takin' the pictures. Shoot!"

I'm screaming, but I'm shooting too, thinking if I take enough pictures he might move in time and the barrelling truck is getting bigger an' nearer an' louder an' I'm shouting at Hank, an' he's shoutin' at me.

"Take the fuckin' photo. Take the shot, take the shot!"

And I do.

He's lying off centre, dead, dead still and he's swallowed under the blare of the horn, the roarin' engine and the grindin' trailer while I scream white into ice air and Hank dices with the edge, right up to it, right to the very damn edge.

And I'm still screaming though there's no-one to hear. I'm screaming his name and screaming his name and my knees buckle under me and I'm pounding the road with my fists and feeling the wet on my face and seeing I'm just one more bit of grit in the snow when Hank stands up, whistling and whooping, so loud and alive I hold my hands over my ears, wanting the snow to bury me and all my damn fear and shame.

This is the only picture I kept. The one of the bike alone in the road. It don't stop me seeing the others—the road slick as oil, ice brittle trees, and Hank, lyin' there. Off centre, disruptive for sure.

ANNUS HORRIBILIS

(1985 Fiat Strada)

When the Fiat breaks down—as it often does—I think, in my bad luck, I might be lucky. Stuck in a no-parking zone but right opposite a garage with the reassurance of engine oil and whining-pop air-torque wrenches.

Maybe my presumption—they will help me, a woman stuck on her own—results in my failure. Maybe they can see I can't pay. Or they're repelled by my desperation.

I leave a note under the wipers, a hopeless appeal to the uniformed attendants, so quick to issue parking fines.

'Broken down. Gone for help.'

I run off to find a phone, wondering who I can call? Who haven't I called upon recently for a favour?

#

We bought the Fiat at a night-time car auction beside Wandsworth Bridge. We sat, cash ready on tiered bleachers while the cars paraded, engines revving, and gears rearing like rodeo horses. Scott suspected cowboys, but I admired the swaggering mechanics, became excited by the bang of a misfiring engine and slamming car doors. Scott watched hawk-eyed as brake lights sparked in the dark, and a flicked wrist fired slashing windscreen wipers.

We bid on viewing, a five-minute hustling. I persuaded Scott to take a chance on hope, luck, and assumption. My expectation soared high as carrion birds, though for £200 it was too good to be true. And sure, the car was a wreck. A metallic blue Fiat Strada banger.

A week later, we drove it to Wales. Two hundred miles from London, a pound for every one of them. When we left the motorway, taking the slip road towards Swansea Bay, only two gears were functioning, second and fourth.

"Jeez," Scott said, "if any more gears go, we'll have to drive backwards."

Scott left me soon afterwards, in a failure of hope and a breakdown of faith and trust—this time, in me. I expected and assumed too much of him and blamed my own failures on other people, missed chances and bad luck.

\#

The Fiat breaks down during the hiatus between my arrest for drunk driving and the start of a 12-month ban with a fine I can't pay. The charge, like the loss of the car, like everything else, I don't think is my fault. I offered to drive, as sober chauffeur for buzzed-up friends. But I hadn't eaten all day, and the one pint I justified turned into at least two while the band played in the sweaty pub, and my friends overheated as fast as their eyes dilated. I drove too fast into a speed trap in Putney. Breathalysed in the shocking cold night air, I was lucky not to be done for more. For the stash stowed by one friend under the passenger seat.

My prints were taken, rolled in staining black ink by a handsome cop who held my fingers in his.

"Those your friends?" he asked, nodding towards them. He sucked his teeth and told me I was unlucky.

#

I return alone to where the Fiat broke down within twenty minutes, but the car is gone. I never see it again. I can't afford to pay the fine to retrieve it.

The gap where it should be is large enough for me to stand in and walk around. It's an odd sensation—being in my car's space without it. It's a small car, but it leaves a vacancy, emptier for the lack of something inside it. There is no point in searching. A car is not dropped like a ring in a gutter or blown like a letter to flitter in the wind. A car isn't lost amongst leaves and litter or thrown out by mistake. A car is towed or driven away.

I shout and glare at the men in the garage opposite, but my fury slides off their oily faces. Later, I wonder if they were in on it. If Clapham Manor Street is a lucrative side earner, being just off the High Road where chancers might park for a five-minute dash—short of time or cash or common sense. I wonder if the men in the garage tip off the parking attendants or summon the tow trucks to swoop like vultures from the Battersea pound.

Standing in the space where the car should be, I'm glad I don't know what else is coming in the months ahead:

hepatitis from surfing in storm swell in Cornwall; the attack by the man who forces his way into my flat; the broken toe where I kick him. The divorce.

I fill the car space with my anger at having no one to blame, and I look for what isn't there—another chance, passive forgiveness. I see my note, crumpled, discarded on the side of the road. I fail to recognise the truth of the few words I wrote. Broken down. Need help.

FORD IMPALA, A CAR FOR GROWN MEN
(1976 Ford Chevrolet Impala)

That was some cruising car. Your cousin Lou was a big man, even for an Islander, but he could have star fished on the buffed bonnet and there still would have been room for you and me. Without touching the shined-up chrome.

We had ice cream sodas, all taking deep drags on our straws. The three of us up front on the bench seat, wider than our sofa. You and Lou, fat-arming out the windows, a one-handed drive.

You fingered my shoulder. I was fourteen.

V8 throbbing north over the harbour bridge and way below, the pointy teeth white sails of cruising yachts, pricking the sea far out into the Hauraki Gulf.

We turned right after the bridge, the car cornering like a stingray in a wide sweeping turn, tracing the north side of the harbour.

Lou said you could drive if you liked. My stomach knotted. Could you handle such a car? Would Lou then finger my shoulder?

He pulled the hand brake from the dash and the two of you swapped sides.

We climbed Mount Victoria at such an acute angle that I could only see the sky. Like I was reclining, and my legs were waving, dangling in the air. A slow rising upwards. The Impala swollen the full width of the road and wound for lift off with the sun sparking off metal.

At the top, levelled out, there was no space for that car. Like we'd landed on a pinhead, with no room to turn around. No room at all.

We balanced there, sucking in the 360 view. City downtown, ferry boats and two iron-grey frigates, Rangitoto, Takapuna beach, out to Motuihe and Mototapu islands and the blue. The shining, crisp blue sea.

Just there. Suspended, afraid to come back down.

ONE LITTLE APPLE CAME TUMBLING DOWN
(1966 Austin A35)

Sophie doesn't like the people who walk too close by. The ones who look and see she's alone. She presses the button locks on the doors, front and back.

Mummy has made her wait in the car. Mummy doesn't like to pay for parking. Mummy watches her pennies. "Just five minutes. I won't be long. Try to be a good girl."

Sophie counts to sixty. She knows there are sixty seconds in a minute. She counts to sixty, five times, raising her fingers, but Mummy doesn't return. Sophie counts again as she might have counted too fast the first time, but she gets muddled, decides she's counted enough.

Sophie opens her colouring book. She picks a red crayon and colours in a picture of a house. One with a door in the middle and a path leading to it, a window either side and a wavy thatched roof. A pretty house where nice people would live. Sophie scribbles, pressing hard and colouring outside of the lines.

Sophie sings to herself. The song she hums when she doesn't want to feel afraid.

Five little apples so red and bright were dancing about on a tree one night.

She sings to her dolly, then shouts and throws Dolly on the floor for being naughty.

"Silly Dolly," she shouts. "You're always under my feet."

Sophie climbs into the front of the car, stepping on the hand brake. She pretends to drive. *Vroom, Vroom.* She wiggles the steering wheel, turning it as far as it will go from side to side. She presses buttons and flicks switches. She flips the windscreen wipers and winds the windows down and up again. *Vroom, Vroom.*

Mummy is saving her pennies in her post office account. She makes the housekeeping stretch. She buys cheap cuts and day-old bread. Mummy sews and darns or buys clothes from the Shelter. Mummy needs money of her own to buy things for herself. To fund her escape.

Sophie slides her bottom in the seat to touch her feet on the pedals, then pulls herself back up and presses on a handle to look up in the mirror. She draws on lipstick with a crayon, puckering her mouth and smacking her lips like Mummy.

She doesn't notice at first when the car starts to move.

The wind came rustling through the town,
One little apple came tumbling down.

LANCE
(1979 Ford Falcon Sprint)

When Lance puts his foot down, the girls try hard not to squeal. Not to take a sharp *'aah-urgh'* intake of breath, because they suspect that Lance likes it.

Lance speeds, slides, and swerves, drives like there's no chance of hazard ahead. The girls press fear in their feet when they will him to brake but if they shout at Lance to slow down, he just smiles and drives faster so they keep their fear to themselves.

"Lance, you're one mad fuck," say his mates but they don't stop him either.

The mates are not much as mates go, but Lance has the wheels and without him there's nowhere to get to. The girls don't like Lance, but they ride with him for the same reason.

Out at Kawhia beach, where they light the fire, share bottles and clump under blankets, Lance sucks his lager, drinks like its water, and stays outside of the firelight.

The girls feel him watching and waiting. Sometimes they see he hunkers in the crumbling slip side like he's disguising himself in early burial. When the girls need to piss in the sand dunes, they always go hand in hand. None of them says it, but none of them wants to go on their own.

None of them says they're surprised when Lance is arrested, convicted, and sent to Mt Eden. That girl from the big smoke thought she knew her way round, but she didn't know no one, didn't know Lance and, big mistake, drove with him solo.

The guys shrug off their guilt like the clothes they've grown out of. They wanted Lance's wheels more than they wanted to stop him.

The girls think they're wiser now that Lance's mates all have cars of their own. '*Aah-urgh*' they say. And sometimes they squeal.

TAILBACK
(2019 Skoda Fabia Estate)

They sail into the back of the queue, blown there on a dying wind to sit becalmed on a sea of tarmac. Stationary, they both still face forward, staring at the car in front, glimpsing the other cars, vans, and trucks in front again, relentlessly repeating, forming a rainbow line of metallic paint, where the motorway leans to the west. They don't know what lies at the end of the rainbow—a crash or roadworks, a spilled load or sheer weight of traffic.

She fiddles with the radio, searching channels for news, hears the report of a vehicle fire, smoke billowing, closing the road miles ahead, stranding them, beached between two far apart junctions.

"Hours" she says. "They say it's going to be hours." She slumps, resigned, settles in for the wait. "At least we have snacks and water. We won't be starving."

He grunts and watches the oncoming traffic on the eastbound carriage way. He envies their motion, senses the drivers' glee to be travelling away, headed in the opposite direction.

She studies the cars marooned alongside. A family of four, plump faced children cushioned in pillows, bikes in decreasing sizes screwed to a brace on the back. One wheel keeps turning, has found some propulsion, its spokes whirring clockwise turning reflective safety discs. She wonders if they always cycle together or if there's a straggler who gets left behind.

"You know they use recycled glass to make roads? Don't drink and drive they say but it's more like drink, or you won't drive. We'll have earnt a bottle or two by the time we get there. If we ever do."

She knows how roads are made, but she titters to show appreciation, like he expects.

He counts the number of cars with single occupants, stops when he reaches one hundred. He starts again counting red cars, becomes bored, and counts yellow cars instead. A driver waves from his window, perhaps in sympathy but it feels like a two fingered salute.

She sees a van billowing cigarette smoke from its open window. The van is jiggling on its suspension. The driver's hand is slapping the door, keeping time to a beat she can't hear.

"Someone looks happy," she says pointing. He grunts again and yawns.

"Do you want something to eat?"

"How can you be hungry already?"

"Well, it's something to do," she says popping open a bag of prawn cocktail crisps. She offers them to him, but he waves her away.

She listens to a play on the radio. He loses track of the plot.

He closes his eyes, pretends he's asleep. She gives way and pretends he's asleep too.

He sits upright after a while to stop his mind drifting towards intersections. Theirs resulted in two children, now following roads of their own.

She taps their residents parking sticker. It's curling at the edges, and she licks her finger, tries to press it back down.

He worries about maintaining heat in the car. Whether the radio is running the battery down, if this waiting will result in mechanical failure, a lay-by breakdown, or a scrap metal heap. Stranded in this no-man's land of immobile traffic where there's nowhere to go to and nowhere to return to, he hears every second, the tick tick ticking in the slow passage of time.

Ahead of them horns start blaring, people are stepping out of their cars, banging roofs, and whistling. All around them, drivers start sounding their horns too, protesting abandonment, finding something collective to do.

"I think it means we might be moving soon," she says.

He shakes his head and opens his door. He steps out of the car leaving the key in the ignition. She watches him weave through the vehicles and bend forward to climb the grass bank on the verge. He straddles the fence at the top and sits there for a moment, a grey man in a grey jacket, then he slides down and disappears into the forlorn autumn trees.

DRIVEN TO IT
(2013 AUDI A3 8P SPORTBACK)

Today, like every weekday morning, at 7.45, she unlocks Car.
But before laying her coat in the back, slinging her bag in the
passenger side, she heaves a suitcase into the boot. Car sinks
with the dead weight.

She slumps in the driver's seat, and locks herself in.
Car hears her sigh like she usually does. Car thinks the sigh
signals relief. When she side-swipes hair from her eyes, plugs
in her seatbelt, the sigh, a release of tightly held breath,
means here I am, I am safe at last. But today her sigh is
pained like she's hurting, slammed by a gut punch or bruised.

The keyring jangles by her knees, ornaments hanging.
Colourful tassels, an emergency whistle, a silver fish hooked
through its mouth. A saint painted in red enamel on a scallop
shaped disc, a plastic shard, printed with numbers for rescue,
by the R.A.C.

Car thinks she cares, but she's either too busy or too
distracted. Water bottles knock and roll in the footwells.
Wrappers, tissues, plasters, and painkiller blister-packs stuff
the side pockets. Car wants a wash, to be rid of the sticky
pollen, mud and spent insects—these are constant irritations—
but there aren't any dents, dings, or scratches. Not on car.

When she's contained inside, Car senses her mood.
Irritable if they're stuck in a stationary queue, joyful on an
empty country road far from home. Car feels her aggression in
acceleration, determination in swift gear changes, frustration
in slammed braking, fear in the snatched glances behind. Car

hears her in the music she plays; slow, sonorous, or thumping, booming loud and fast, fast, fast.

Car waits, wondering why she's not yet ready to start.

She fumbles with her keys. The tassels and trinkets fall through her fingers, and she scrabbles by her feet to retrieve them. She manages to put the key in the ignition but still they don't move. Car realises she is crying; her eyes are swollen. She can't see to drive. She lays her head on the hard steering wheel.

She sobs.

Car waits.

She finds a tissue to wipe her eyes, blows her nose, a snorting wet blast. She starts the engine but stalls.

Car winces.

She starts again, makes a three-point turn like she's crossing herself and turns Car west out of town. They take short cuts and zip, reduced into lanes to make way for buses and bicycles. They turn at roundabouts and pass under flyovers until they're joining the Friday exodus, the cut up and rumble of traffic, as it positions and manoeuvres, barely restrained, a herd of wild horsepower, penned and constricted by sheer weight of traffic. Speed cameras flash their sinister warnings along miles of roadworks and multiple lane closures, and the slow progress reveals the litter of travellers, commuters, and couriers, hurled as quoits among traffic cones, or flung, forlorn, onto median strips.

Beyond the restrictions she slams her foot to the floor and sings, bluesy and mournful to the radio. Car roars past scrubby side verges, past split plastic bottles and tossed paper bags, lost in the whip-whining cry of fast traffic.

Car hears her voice become harsh and ugly. She shouts, rasping curses, and turns up the volume. She opens the windows to let the wind reel and whirl. She drives faster and Car knows she's past caring. She's not checking her mirrors, watching for speed cameras, or minding other drivers. She's straddling the lanes, driving like she owns the whole damned highway, like she's queen of the tarmac, the smart centre of the motorway. She owns the road and races like she's flying and free.

Car sees the end of the road in a flip or an oil slick, a spin, or a skid. Driven to it, Car sparks with inspiration, fires with resolve and finds her final answer, choosing combustion, licks of once passionate flames, a blazing sacrifice like her keyring saint's martyrdom, scorching caresses from under the burnt-out hot bonnet.

PLAYING CHICKEN ON THE GUADAJOZ ROAD
(1985 BMW318i & 1989 Toyota MR2)

She drives by the walled cemetery with its silent Madonna's and plastic flower bouquets, turns out onto the Guadajoz road. Driving like she's some pro.

He's not yet in view but she knows he's behind her. That car, sweeping dirt, back end sliding out on corners. She leaves town for dust thrown by the unsealed road, drives through husky fields where wild orchids stud the calloused clay banks.

She'd seen him fold his limbs into his silver car—parked like she hoped, like she expected outside bar La Cueva—but kept her eyes straight ahead. She'd slowed to be sure, then knew he'd seen her, would be following her soon. Out beyond the desolate pueblo, where bunker white buildings stare blindly from visor slit windows, and dominoes no longer slap tables in the one bleak bar.

No one goes there, no one goes further, no one goes to the house they found years ago, hidden by cresting palm trees, its ruined walls secreted in blazing shocks of pink bougainvillea.

Aircon off, windows down and summer lashing, snatching her hair. Music and the thrumming motor, boom-box and stereo sound.

She sees him in her mirror, drawing nearer, and teases her foot down, listening to the revs as she slips through the gears.

He's getting closer.

She releases some pressure—she won't brake to slow down—allows him to gain on her. He rams his horn in salute riding up close to her bumper. He pulls on his wheel, swings out and comes along side, cocked out of his window, just like before, grinning at her and sounding his horn blast again.

Hot air both in and out, they lock on each other's faces. Dead pan then laughing like teenagers again. She squeezes her foot down not looking ahead, just looking at him, knowing she's wild eyed, that her mouth is wide open.

The cars side by side, silver and blue on the longest straight of the narrow dirt road. Tense and gripping, fighting for control. Faster now with dust like fury behind them, the road closing so soon, the tight bend racing towards them, a stand of poplar trees marking the curve, silent judges on a finishing line.

Ten, nine, eight seconds—there's no time left but they dare. Dare to drive like there's all the time in the world for them, all the space on the road to keep racing, onwards, side by side. Seven, six, five. Speed, wind, and heat but no time at all. Four, three, two...

Reckless, on the edge and hot crazy with it. She never felt so alive.

LUCKY FAT FUCK
(1987 Kawasaki GPZ900r Ninja)

If the stop-start traffic had been lighter, if he'd been going faster, his flight and slide would have been longer.

Force defined by Newton's second law of motion: distance equals speed multiplied by time.

When he braked too hard because swerving wasn't an option, he felt himself fly. In free forward motion, high on the flyover bridge. In the moment, a part second interlude, he saw the sea, blue as it should be and the clear sky where one cumulus cloud suggested a soft-landing.

Greg knows his propulsion was like a boulder flung from a trebuchet or a cannon ball shot. He remembers shutting his eyes to the beckoning cloud, remembers the blue shaded, became gravel black.

"You're one lucky fat fuck," Shane says again.

Greg gives his sideways smile where half his mouth stays rigid and his top lip curls in the corner. He leans back on the stacked hospital pillows, trying to hide his grimace.

If he'd swerved, he'd have hit oncoming traffic. Greg squeezes his eyes and kneads the sheets with his fingers.

Collision: a release of kinetic energy, louder, hotter, and messier.

Shane is talking again. Greg watches Shane's mouth move but wonders if the siren scrape of his helmet on tarmac, a tinnitus ringing tin-tin, has affected his hearing. He doesn't need Shane to tell him he's one lucky fat fuck. Greg knows all the ifs. He's not stupid.

In truth Greg was briefly airborne before he slid like a summer-sleek penguin. A slide on tarmac that burned holes in his jeans and sliced layers from his belly where his leather jacket rode up.

If he'd not looked at the view, not gazed at the sea, his reactions might have been quicker.

50 kms an hour equals 13.88 metres per second.

Greg calculates; a stop just one metre short of the concrete camber lip.

55 kms an hour equals 15.27 metres per second.

If he'd had some girl riding pillion, clutching his waist, squeezing his hips with her thighs, excited and shrieking in his ear…Greg weighs up the odds. He scored on boots versus sneakers, gloves, and helmet of course. He lost on jeans, scored on fat over thin. Greg calculates density, mass, and gravitational pull.

"So," Shane is saying. "You mean, if you were not so fat, you would have spilt your guts? Like sausages?"

"Yeah mate. Like sausages."

Epidermis, dermis, hypodermis.

Greg sees his skin peeled, pared like pale pink onion rings. He wonders how many layers can be taken before nothing remains. He calculates saviour in calories. In burgers, thick shakes, and pies.

The speed limit on the flyover is 100 km per hour. A limit Greg often treats as a guideline.

27.77 metres per second.

Flight, collision, motion, and heat. A meteor, a fallen star, knocked off its transit, molten rock plunged, to hiss in the chilling blue sea.

"You're one lucky fat fuck," Shane says yet again.

"Yeah, so you keep saying. Mate, you can fuck off unless you're going to get me something decent to eat."

"Sure bro. What d'ya want?"

Greg considers his options, knows Shane is keen to be helpful. He starts to think about food but finds himself thinking about the girl who might have been riding pillion and about the road and what if it had been slippery with greasy rain or falling sharply downhill?

"Ah you know what? I'm not hungry. Stay here a while but talk about something else." Greg watches Shane, sees he's struggling for something to say. "You know, bands, movies, the footie. Anything."

He leans back and waits; watches Shane's mouth start moving again. He hears the ringing tin-tin in his ears and lets himself sink, deep, deep into the clouds of his pillows.

DAZZLED BY THE BRILLIANCE
(2014 Seat Ibiza)

It's in the moment of blindness. The children buckled asleep in the back on top of sand-crusted towels, mouths slack and heads lolling within their protective seats. Her husband asleep too, fully relaxed.

Leaving the long dark tunnel faster than her eyes can adjust, she is too slow in flapping the visor against the bloody-red sun. The miracle of seeing again occurs too late and she slams the brakes too hard, swerves too far onto the wrong side of the road.

It's no longer a bikini knot prodding her back or salt crisping her hair. It's not her sandals rubbing her heels or sunburn blistering her skin.

In a suspended moment before never seeing again, she pictures the children splashing in clear shallow water, the debris left on the table after a long lazy lunch. She hears the satisfied sigh as her husband lies back on the sun lounger, warm, content, and replete.

The August sun sets to purple sheer arid peaks, and the sapphire sea deepens from blue to blue-black. Shadows darken the gorges and silver-green slivers of broom wave a gentle, tender farewell. And the grapefruit moon rises, brimming large with unbearable longing. Bigger than the blazing sun has been all the slow day.

HILUX INVINCIBLE
(2010 Toyota Hilux Ute)

I'm climbing the cliff path. I'm slow because I'm carrying a bit of weight, and while I am fitter than I was, I won't win any races. Still, I'm jogging. Uphill. A little giddy, which happens sometimes. A lightness to the head, a loss of time and place.

To my right, the drop is sheer. The rhythmic sea sluices on the rocks below and I use the swish, wisp, pause and thunder to measure my pace and breathing. *Huff, two, three, four. Puff, two, three, four.*

I think of myself as a diesel Hilux Ute—'she's a bit battered but tough and reliable.' Not flash or fast but can overcome every obstacle. When I see runners whip past, sleek like sports cars, I think—they are the type to get shin splints, to snap an Achilles tendon.

I have time on my hands. Or perhaps I should say, I have time on my feet. Ousted, redundant, undermined. Replaced by a mint newer model, a winner of races.

Above me, I catch a flash of yellow, maybe a coat of someone coming down from the higher viewpoint.

I am halfway up when he rides over the brow—a stunted blonde boy on a plastic push-along toy car. The path narrows, and the boy in his yellow raincoat is moving fast, gaining speed with the downward momentum. I look around, surprised by the oddness—a boy alone at his age—but there is no one else in sight.

I can hear the rumble grind of the wheels on the path, and I stand aside for him to pass by safely.

He's coming too fast, and I call out, "Careful. Use your feet, slow down!"

The path is steep banked on the hill side. Behind me the cliff falls away. I shout, "Stop! Watch out!" but he keeps coming quickly.

The boy holds the centre line then veers towards me, steers right at me. I step back into the scree, but I can't retreat any further. I'm still shouting, screaming now, and the boy is almost upon me.

I'm right on the edge when he rams me. I brace to the slam in my shins. I lean into the pain, or I will slip over the edge. I grab his hands on the black plastic wheel, try to wrestle him back down the path. He gurns, pawing hard at the ground with rubber booted feet. Snarling, he growls, trying to push with his legs.

My shoes are sliding, and I use all my strength to resist him. He keeps shoving and straining, his face is livid, puce with effort.

"Stop you little Shit! Stop, you're pushing me. You'll push me over you little Fucker!"

I surprise him when I twist. I roar and rotate like a discus thrower, strong, muscular, using my weight as ballast to hurl him high and over to smash, yellow flash, on the sea-washed rocks below.

I look and listen. I see the path is empty, in both directions. A few cawing gulls' whirl and turn in the sky. Baaing sheep keep grazing on the hill above me, and the simmering sea stretches clear to the horizon. I hear the swish, wisp, pause, and thunder of waves.

I straighten my clothing, wipe my brow, and slow my breath. I turn, and run, finding a new gear. I run with swift, athletic bounce, climbing, leaping, sprinting like a winner to the peak of the coastal path.

PUMPING AT PIHA
(1970 VW Beetle 1303)

The cicadas hum. The warm air smells of recent rain. We drive west, climbing the Waitaks, blinking through summer shadows as the narrow road carves through deep bush. We listen to Icehouse thinking it's cool. Thinking we're cool in the blue VW Beetle with boards on the roof.

From the viewpoint high above Piha, we watch the sets forming, can see the spray curling backwards, so white against the blue, blue water, and the black, black sand. You study the rip, the fast calm running beside and behind Lion Rock, and we hear the boom and retort of the thumping surf and know it's going to be a big day.

We drive off fast, impatient to bury our feet in hot sand, to feel the gasp of cold water.

And the day is big. The waves so perfect from above are huge, big mamas, mountainous, powerful, steep, and barrelling and the undertow grabs at our ankles, sucks holes under our feet and you're whooping as you paddle, watching the waves build and crest beside you, cruising the rip out back.

I body surf between the flapping orange flags. Later, I wait on my beach towel, looking for you duck diving or riding in black neoprene, and I panic when I scan the waves and I think I've lost you, frantic until I find you, flicking over the lip to fly from sight again, and I know, in the sharp pang of possible loss, I love you.

You might have kissed me. With salt still clinging to your lashes, and water dripping from your hair. If you'd returned, you might have bent low to greet me, waiting there on my damp yellow towel in the black, black sand. I can pretend you loved me too. More than the siren call of the treacherous singing sea

LANE ASSIST
(2015 Peugeot 2008 Automatic)

Mike is not keen on automatics. It's not real driving, he says. "I like to be in control of my own gear changes. Especially in a hire car, when I'm not paying for the servicing!" He gives Jean a nudge-nudge, assuming her approval, reminding her again, he pays.

But for the amount he's prepared to spend on their holiday hire, his options are limited. He presents his licence and signs the forms with a flourish like they're lucky to have him.

Mike is not perturbed by left-hand drive. He doesn't mind driving abroad. He knows the roads between the airport and the villa they return to every year. He knows the road over the mountain, the way to the beach, the Carrefour turn off, the route to the one restaurant he likes.

On the mountain road Mike likes to drive fast, ignoring Jean's pleas to slow down. He challenges himself on twists and bends and accelerates, listening to the automatic transition, gears changing with the steep incline. He drifts across lanes on the first hairpin bend to find the smooth driving line, feels the tug of resistance in the wheel, sees a flash on the dashboard, hears the *'beep beep beep'* alarm.

"Bloody Lane Assist. Turn it off will you. I hate a car telling me what to do."

"It's because you didn't indicate."

"There's no one to indicate to woman!"

"The car doesn't know that."

"Find the bloody button. I won't be told what to do."

Mike tuts while Jean searches for the corresponding button to press. The *'beep beep beep'* sounds again.

"Turn it off!"

"I have. I pressed it."

"Press again. I can't look while I'm driving. It's hard enough with the sun in my eyes."

The shrill *'beep beep beep'* sounds on every excursion. Mike shouts and wrestles with the car, shouts at Jean but refuses to let her drive.

He makes her study the manual, tells her to google for advice. "Lane Assist," she reads out, "is a safety feature designed to stop accidents caused when a car drifts out of lane – perhaps due to a lapse of concentration or drowsiness – by warning you of your impending doom."

"Impending doom? It's just bloody annoying. You'd think if it was that bad, they'd have some siren, or blimmin' great drums or...I don't know, tolling bells!"

#

Mike wakes to find the villa too quiet. He pads into the kitchen, looks in the bathroom then steps outside, shading his eyes on the sun lit terrace. He calls Jean's name. He calls again and again, irritation snagging his voice.

Inside he finds the note on the glass coffee table where the car keys should be. Where he threw them the night before. The note is a terse, one line message.

'Listen to your voicemail.'

Mike stares at his phone in confusion. He dials 121. He holds the phone to his ear and listens. All he can hear is *'Beep, beep, beep.'* A message of impending doom.

THE SUN STILL INSISTS UPON RISING
(2009 Kawasaki Z 1000)

If today you had ridden up onto Great Bentley Green to join the park up and pints and the 'alright?', 'alright? with the slaps on the back, then they'd clear the hot pasties and curling sandwiches, remove the brownies and small custard squares and The Plough would serve drinks from enough real glasses like it was any other bloody day.

If today we could undo yesterday and the countless bleak, black days of suffering in the dark months before, you might find some comfort in the acceptance of greyness. Grey like the blokes' three-day stringy beards and their worn fraying t-shirts and the endless, stretching, high Essex skies.

If today, you'd seen the cavalcade of Coggeshall Bastards strapped in their leathers, strung together by long thinning hair and the inky lines of their full body tats. If today you'd seen their throbbing-engine parade when they came to salute you, but couldn't all shoulder into the crem, then you might have decided to ride again alongside them instead of leading the pack.

If today, we could undo yesterday, you'd see the sun still insists upon rising. Even when the days are clouded over or become too wild and windswept, or when the rain flies in slap-sideways, the sun—it still insists upon rising.

If today you'd seen the sorrow when we gathered to mourn the spaces where you should be, and the places you should be going to—all the journeys left to be taken—you might have paused. Or hesitated.

If today, you'd seen the heads of coloured dahlias replicating your electric guitar, and the card sending love to the missing Legendary Character, you might have heard the songs still to sing and the recordings still to make. You might have booked the band for all the gigs left to play.

If tomorrow we can fix all the yesterdays, you will wear your biking jacket, and laugh your bass-line joke. You will sit astride your grunting bike on the butt hard unforgiving seat. You'll sling your guitar across your shoulder and ride off to smack freedom full in the fucking face.

And though the sun still insists upon rising, every morning, the days will be longer, emptier and greyer, and you'll still leave us far, far behind.

PREVIOUSLY PUBLISHED STORIES

HANGAR STRAIGHT
Fictive Dream, 16th September 2022

KISSING IN A BOTTLE GREEN JAGUAR
Fairfield Scribes Micro Fiction, October 2022

PLUCKY BACKPACKERS IN THE LYNMOUTH FLOOD
The Phare, June 2022

AIRCOOLED VW BAJA
Retreat West, December 2021 Runner Up

IN THE CANNON OF BEECH TREES
Reflex Fiction 11th July 2021 (under the title Stopping The Morris Traveller)

ANNUS HORRIBILIS
Ellipsis Zine, July 2022 (under title Annus Horribilis and a Blue Fiat Strada)

FORD IMPALA, A CAR FOR GROWN MEN
Reflex Fiction, 9th April 2021

ONE LITTLE APPLE CAME TUMBLING DOWN
Roi Fainéant, September 2022

DAZZLED BY BRILLIANCE
Flash Frontier, March 26th, 2023

PUMPING AT PIHA
Free Flash Fiction, Highly Commended Sept 2022

THE SUN STILL INSISTS UPON RISING
Free Flash Fiction, August 2021

AKNOWLEDGEMENTS

The idea for this collection came to me in New Zealand when I was wide-eyed with jetlag in the small hours. The first car story I had published was Ford Impala (thank you Reflex Fiction) and I became obsessed with stories about cars and journeys. There's something unique about being in an enclosed space while moving. Often conversations can be more revelatory, and experiences can be heightened when speed and motion come into play.

I owe a huge debt to Future Learn's Start Writing Fiction course which kickstarted me into action after a writing hiatus of decades, and to Matt Kendrick who steered me through this collection and saved me from many wrong turns. A few of the stories spluttered into life on his brilliant Lyrical Writing course. I'm so grateful for his insightful wisdom. He's the most patient driving instructor.

Special mention to Beta Readers Association (B.R.A), all stunning writers, Maria Thomas, Joyce Bingham and Hilary Ayshford for their uplifting support, honest, constructive feedback, and most importantly, their friendship.

Thanks also to the wonderful communities of Globe Soup and SWF and especially Retreat West and Writers HQ where some of these stories started. The feedback I have received on their forums from so many exceptional, inspirational Flash writers has been invaluable. And thank you to Michael Loveday for the guidance on his site and for writing his excellent book 'Unlocking the Novella in Flash'.

Thank you to my parents who first taught me to drive in a noisy, underpowered, mustard-coloured Austin Maxi 1100 and to my precious family and friends for the journeys we've had and the ones yet to come.

Cover Art: E J H T Mackenzle

Emily Macdonald was born in England but grew up in New Zealand.

She has won and been placed in several writing competitions, including a shortlisting in the Bath Short Story Award 2023. She has work published by Fictive Dream, Reflex Fiction, Retreat West, Lucent Dreaming, Crow & Cross Keys, Ellipsis Zine, Roi Fainéant, Free Flash Fiction and The Phare amongst others.

Twitter: ek_macdonald

Bluesky: @ekmacdonald.bsky.social

Links to her published writing can be found here: https://www.macdonaldek11.com

Printed in Great Britain
by Amazon

33113305R00037